Grooming Longhaired Cats
Basic Cat Grooming Techniques

By Svetlana Broussova

First published in Great Britain 2015
by Cat Grooming School Ltd
www.catgroomingschool.co.uk

Copyright © 2013 Svetlana Broussova

ISBN 978-0-9933636-3-4

Printed in Great Britain by Outside the Box
www.outsidethebox.org.uk

Designed by Detroit Design
www.detroitdesign.co.uk

The brands of products illustrated are not exclusively endorsed by the author. Alternative products are available

Disclaimer: the author cannot be held responsible for any injuries sustained by cat groomers following any of the techniques outlined in this book

Dedication

I dedicate this book to the most important person in my life – my daughter Vera Broussova. You are the most incredible, talented and wonderful young lady. You are my complete and total inspiration, the meaning of my life and a huge encouragement. You are my best friend and the best child in the world! I am so proud of you!

Acknowledgements

I would like to say a huge thank you to:

Edita Urbonaite, for her amazing assistance in every respect of my business, for her kind heart, caring personality, hardworking attitude, amazing friendship and constant support. My most profound gratitude goes to her;

James Hogan, for his incredible and tireless hard work, dedicated to animal welfare around the world. For his friendship and amazing support whenever I have needed it;

Charlotte Melville, editor, for her talent, great interest and assistance in making my dream come true;

Leslie Potter-Withers, our book designer, for her patience, love and dedication to her job;

Julie Crosby, our print co-ordinator, for her passion and great organisation;

Natalja Kondratova, a very special friend, for her invaluable and continuous encouragement and support;

Mr and Mrs Gordon, the wonderful caring parents of our model Persian cats Elvis and Priscilla. For their love, support and great patience;

All my lovely friends and family, fantastic employees, amazing students and the professionals who cherish, inspire and assist me.

To my readers: I truly hope you enjoy my book!

Praise for the Author

"The skills required to be a successful cat groomer are many and varied. Prerequisites include: using the appropriate materials and equipment in a sensitive, professional manner; understanding the behavioural traits and psychology of the individual animals being groomed so that they are helped to feel as relaxed as possible; as well as inspiring confidence in the owners so that they are reassured by the standard of care provided for their pet. These are just a few of the essential requirements for success in the grooming business, all with the objective of ensuring that the finished result achieves the winning combination of a happy, handsome animal and an equally happy, satisfied customer.

Finding these skills in one person is a big ask but Svetlana Broussova surely has them in abundance, skills she has honed and refined through her years of experience as the proprietor of Pet Universe pet grooming salon. The passion and commitment she brings to her work has made her one of the most successful practitioners in her field.

The professional Cat Grooming School Ltd was created by Svetlana to enable students to reach the highest professional standard, taking the students on a rigorous and comprehensive journey from first principles through to final outcomes.

With her warm, vibrant personality and excellent communication skills, Svetlana gives the same energy and commitment to her training course as she does to her grooming business. I believe that no one is better equipped than Svetlana Broussova to convey to students the essentials of cat grooming, providing them with the necessary training, expertise and confidence to help them make a success of their chosen career."

James Hogan has worked to improve the welfare of animals at home and abroad for over 40 years. In that time he has served as vice chairman of a branch of the RSPCA, been chairman of an animal rehoming centre and organised training programmes for animal care workers in places as far afield as Russia. He is currently serving as a trustee of an American animal charity working to rescue stray animals in Afghanistan.

"It was only a matter of time before Svetlana put her energies into writing about her unique approach to cat grooming, one which I have greatly admired and strived to do proud myself.

She taught me invaluable understanding of a cat's behaviour, which enabled me to develop and empathy with the cat, alongside firmness and control, so that a happy medium is found and the groom can be completed as humanely and peacefully as possible. I have not found this method in any other grooming establishment, which only highlights Svetlana's absolute passion and dedication to doing the right thing for the cats in her care, and for her clients who put all of their trust in her when handing their cat over. I am thrilled that a book is being written by the best cat groomer in the UK.

I wish her all the success in the world"

Anita Kelsey, London –
Cat Grooming School Graduate

I visited the Cat Grooming School as I wanted to learn how to groom my two Persian cats, one of whom was rescued and is very nervous. I learned so much from this course – Svetlana gave me invaluable advice on taking care of my cats and I have taken this knowledge home where I can groom my kitties myself. It was also a lovely bonding experience and one that we all enjoyed thoroughly, I would recommend this for any cat owner who would like to groom their cat at home!

Katie Byrne, London –
Cat Grooming School Graduate

There are various schools of thought regarding the technique of cat grooming and what becomes apparent with Svetlana are her very clear and refined ideas on this matter. I found this very important as it gave me a sense of consistency and discipline, which I have carried forward with me into my professional career.

When I trained with Svetlana her course was intense and demanding, but she was always on hand to offer support and assistance. She has the knack of pushing her students to the limits of their potential so they realise just what they are capable of.

Svetlana is a woman of strong character and infectious energy. I found my time at her cat grooming school an extremely useful and informative experience which provided me with the crucial skills required to set up my own business. Moreover, Svetlana has continued to offer me useful guidance and support as my business has evolved.

Sandra Hilton, *Lancashire –*
Cat Grooming School Graduate

Svetlana Broussova,
Author and Director of
Cat Grooming School Ltd

The Author

Svetlana Broussova was born in Azov, Russia, in 1967. From her earliest years
Svetlana knew that she wanted to be a vet – taking care of a menagerie of pets
– and in 1982 she began training as a veterinary nurse at the Novocherkassk
Veterinary College before going on to study at the Don State Agrarian University,
graduating as a veterinary surgeon in 1994. In 1997 she opened her own
veterinary practice in Azov.

Svetlana moved to the UK in 1999. The immediate financial and other demands
of settling in a new country prevented her from following her chosen career but,
undeterred, she found work in related fields, first at the London animal charity,

The Mayhew Animal Home, then later on at the Goddard Veterinary Group and finally, in 2002, as the Animal Welfare Officer at the Harrods Pet Shop department, Knightsbridge.

In 2004, Svetlana set up her own mobile grooming salon – the first cat grooming salon on wheels in the UK – and by 2005 her Pet Universe business had grown into a permanent home in East London.

At the same time Svetlana launched a series of public cat grooming demonstrations. The unprecedented success of her teaching led her to found the Cat Grooming School, which opened its doors to students in 2006 and has been a burgeoning college ever since.

Svetlana lives in London with her fiancé, and their cats, Cristal, Kiara and Snowbell.

The Cat Grooming School

Welcome to the Cat Grooming School and the second professional manual on the rudiments of grooming a longhaired cat.

This book has been written for cat lovers wishing to gain knowledge in professional cat grooming techniques, whether working in a veterinary environment, cattery, rescue centre or simply interested in pursuing a career in this field.

In the UK, there is currently no nationally recognised qualification for cat grooming. This is partly due to the fact that unlike dogs, which are pack animals, cats are more solitary and territorial creatures who will not tolerate being lined up in rows.

Hence, good instruction in cat grooming requires one room for every cat: space which is rarely available in today's often over-crowded college buildings.

As a consequence, there are very few professional cat groomers either operating or teaching in Britain and more often than not, cats that become terrified or aggressive when their owners attempt to groom them, are taken to the vet as a last resort, to be de-matted, de-tangled or to shave off their matted coats or have their claws clipped. This can prove expensive, traumatic and can endanger the health of older cats, if medicinal sedation is employed.

This manual has been designed to provide you with the basic principles of professional cat grooming which will complement the more comprehensive and practical courses offered by the Cat Grooming School.

Established in 2004, the Cat Grooming School, currently based in London, UK, offers a wide range of courses, from a half-day introduction to cat grooming for cat owners to an advanced master class, designed for anyone wishing to establish their own professional practice.

Here we provide expert care for our cats and first-class tuition for our students in a calm and welcoming environment where *cat whispering*, rather than brute force, is the fundamental key to any successful relationship with a cat.

Full details of the courses offered by The Cat Grooming School are available on my website: www.catgroomingschool.co.uk

With best wishes

Svetlana Broussova, 2015

Contents

Introduction   13

Chapter 1:   Getting Equipped   19

Chapter 2:   Setting the Scene   31

Chapter 3:   Bonding with your Cat   33

Chapter 4:   Claw Clipping   37

Chapter 5:   Dry Grooming   49

Chapter 6:   Cleaning the eyes, ears and nose   63

Chapter 7:   Wet Bath   67

Chapter 8:   Drying the Cat   77

Chapter 9:   Re-affirming your Bond with the Cat   83

Elvis, our model.

Introduction

Welcome to the manual for grooming longhaired cats. I hope you will find this book a useful guide to grooming your own cat, or if you are a professional groomer that it offers you some new tips and reinforces the skills that you have already acquired.

One thing to note is that this is most definitely a *guide* – I am not trying to impose techniques, or insist that my methods are the best and the only way to do a good job.

These are just the skills and techniques that we use day in, day out in our cat grooming salon and they work very well for us and our students!

Why do we need a book on cat grooming?

There are lots of points of view on the best positions and handling procedures for grooming. I am often asked by cat owners about the best way to groom their kitties at home, and the Cat Grooming School has more and more students each year! We want to share our best and most effective techniques so everyone can be a good cat groomer.

Occasionally I have met with a professional who has come to the grooming school for a quick lesson to improve their skills and learn more advanced techniques. I love sharing our knowledge, but I have often been deeply upset and worried by what I have seen them do. Poor kitties! This is because there is a lack of information about the appropriate products and cat grooming techniques that are available.

So in this manual we will be showing you a much more humane, loving and fun method of cat grooming. It is based on building a strong and trusting bond with your cat so that he or she allows you to groom them happily, making it a fun process for both of you!!!!!

The real secret of success in any cat grooming story is to be a cat lover! It will make you more in tune to the cat's needs, and the cat will sense your love for him and trust you back!!!

Why do we need to groom our cats?

There are many different types and breed of cats in the world, and most of them have hair. Mother nature made nothing by accident, and gave all animals the characteristics they need to survive and adapt well to their environment – cats need their hair to protect them from the cold, wind and sun and to act as an extra layer of protection against infections and cuts they might get roaming around outside. They need their claws to catch prey and to fight any predators.

A glossy, neat coat is the first indicator of a healthy cat and every cat needs one! **Kittens** are taught to groom themselves from birth. Their mother licks them from top to bottom, massaging the skin and coat – this keeps them clean but also increases the blood circulation, stimulating the hair glands to distribute natural essential oils, vitamins and minerals, keeping the fur shiny and in good condition. But what if the mother was a lazy mother, or the kitten was orphaned? We can encourage his natural instincts for grooming. If the kitten didn't learn from his mother, we can remind him and teach him – even if he is a grownup by the time we find him! The majority of the time, mother should teach them and as humans we should carry on helping them with this natural process.

Outdoor cats shed their coats seasonally. In winter they prepare for the cold with more layers, and in summer they lose their extra layers with the heat. These cats need a strong, clean and healthy coat as it's very important for protection against the weather and diseases. Outdoor cats suffer from hairballs too but they eat grass, a natural emetic, to help pass them. They shed their claws by scratching trees and climbing.

Indoor cats can really use our help with shedding excess fur – because they live in the constant warm environment of a house, they moult all the time. Because they live inside where there are no trees to climb or prey to catch, their claws grow very long. Therefore, it is essential to provide the cat with a scratching post or trim the claws regularly.

When cats lick themselves clean they are particularly prone to getting hairballs. A cat's tongue is covered in tiny, backwards-facing hooks that have several uses – they are there to help the cat grip its food, and they help with grooming. The little barbs on the tongue pull out the hairs easily. Because they face backwards, hair gathers in the mouth and the cat swallows it. If there is an excess of hair, it can form hairballs in the cat's stomach, which can be very uncomfortable and cause constipation.

For indoor cats, getting rid of the hairballs may require an expensive visit to the vet for treatment with liquid paraffin.

Overweight cats find it more difficult to reach their tails and backsides, meaning these areas are neglected. Equally though, a **slim cat** can be lazy – so you need to keep an eye on your cat's mannerisms. If he doesn't clean himself you need to teach him!

So with a good grooming regime, you are providing your cat with an essential service:

- You minimise the risk of hairballs
- You can spot abnormal lumps and bumps early, which might even save his life
- You are reducing the risk of him developing a skin condition
- You are boosting the essential oils in his coat, ensuring that he has the best protection possible against cold, rain and infections
- You keep his claws neat and healthy.

It's also a wonderful thing for you too

- It will reduce the amount of hair you find on the sofa and on your clothes!
- It can be a wonderful, therapeutic experience for both you and cat; you will find that your bond grows stronger.

Each breed of cat has *specific* characteristics. For example, some Persian cats have less oil in their fur, so blow-drying the fur is very simple but they benefit from a moisture-rich conditioner. Other breeds, like the Maine Coon, have fur that is already rich in oils, so it takes longer to blow dry, and they don't need extra conditioners. White cats generally seem to find water very frightening and they usually do better with dry grooming. The list goes on – over the Cat Grooming series we will be exploring all of them with you.

But we believe the most important thing, above knowing all the skills, is showing respect for the unique personality of your cat. There will always be more to learn and so much to share, and I'm excited that we are going on this journey together.

Getting Equipped

Chapter 1

What to Wear

Before you begin to groom the cat, it's important to be dressed appropriately.

- It is essential for personal hygiene. On a basic level, it keeps cat hair and dust off your clothes. On a more serious level, if the cat has an infection, wearing uniform will reduce the risk of you catching it.
- As a professional, it makes a good impression on customers to see you in a smart uniform.
- It will reduce cross-contamination between cats. Most of this is common sense – you just want to reduce the spread of infection as much as possible (fleas can be really unpleasant, and ringworm downright dangerous).

For your body

As you start to explore you will find dozens of different brands and styles of uniform available on the market, at a wide range of prices, and it is worth shopping around.

There are some very expensive and beautifully made uniforms out there. However, you need to find a balance between looking professional, maintaining hygiene standards and being cost effective. It is best to wash your uniform at the end of every work-day, to avoid the risk of spreading infection both for yourself and the cats. Therefore, it's good to have one set for each day of the week so that you are not constantly washing clothes! Invest in a good bundle of less expensive overalls – it also helps to cover costs: if you rip the jacket of a £70 pair of overalls it will hurt more to replace!

Look for a durable, nylon fabric that is hair resistant and can stand being washed regularly. Try to avoid anything with pockets – cat hair will find a way in and it's difficult to wash it out. It must be breathable and easy to move around in.

For an additional layer of protection, you can wear a plastic or disposable apron over the top. This is optional, but you may find it a useful extra layer of waterproofing when you bath the cat.

Hair

It's important to tie up long hair, and cover your head with a hair net (something that looks a bit like a shower cap) as cat hair has a habit of sticking to your own hair. On a more serious note, if the cat has ringworm, you can catch it through your hands, as well as through your hair.

Face

When you are brushing and blow-drying the cat, it's sensible to wear goggles, as small dust and hair particles can fly into your eyes and cause irritation. Wear a mask to cover the lower half of your face, to avoid any dust or fur getting into your nose and mouth. Also, in the unlucky event of a cat trying to scratch your face, it will protect you.

Hands

If you use the right technique and gentle approach you shouldn't need much protection for your hands! However, it's a good idea to wear a pair of latex or vinyl gloves. They should be a comfortable fit around your fingers, so that you still maintain a good natural contact with the cat, but thick enough to offer some protection if the cat does try to nip or scratch your hand. This is also a good idea for keeping your hands in general good condition – constant washing and the heat from the blow-dryer will soon dry them out if they're not covered.

Feet

You will often be on your feet at work, so comfortable, non-slip shoes are very important. Avoid open-toed shoes, too – if you drop sharp scissors and heavy clippers by accident, they will protect you.

Of course, if you are only grooming your own cat this is less important.

Tools & Equipment

If you are an experienced cat groomer, you will already know how big and varied the market for pet products is!

There are hundreds of different types and brands of grooming tables, brushes, combs, shampoos, towels etc. produced by dozens of brands. It's a minefield!

You will need:

- Lightweight jacket and trousers, or overalls
- Apron
- Hair net
- Goggles
- Gloves
- Comfortable shoes, that cover your toes

It's often a case of trial and error, and it is worth testing out a range of different brushes and brands until you find the ones that you are most comfortable with – if you are a professional you may already have found a range that you're happy with.

We have also scoured the market for the products we think are best, and we use these daily at the salon.

Table

Grooming a cat is much easier on a flat surface than on a sofa or your lap. There are many tables available on the market, from a standard or simple folding table, to hydraulic and electric height-adjustable ones.

Folding tables are cheap and ideal for mobile cat grooming, they are easy to carry and take up very little space when folded.

The downside is that you cannot adjust the height, but you can start with this and as your business grows you can invest in a better one.

You will need the following equipment and products:

- *Table*
- *Nail clippers*
- *Combs and brushes*
- *Conditioning spray*
- *Ear and eye wipes*
- *Cotton buds*
- *Pair of scissors for any trimming if required*

Sink and shower unit

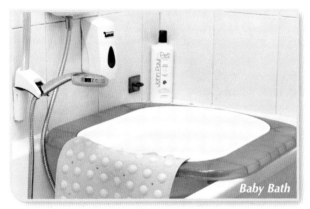

Baby Bath

Hydraulic tables are height adjustable and less expensive than electric ones, but are usually heavy and oversized, with too big a work surface.

An electric table is ideal as you can adjust the height silently and seamlessly while the cat is on it, and it looks more professional. They are expensive but a really worthwhile investment.

If you are grooming at home and don't think a special table is necessary, you can use any other work surface, just place a simple rubber mat down first to give your cat a good grip, and avoid him injuring himself. The choice is yours, all you really need is:

- A small work area (the smaller the better, otherwise you will be chasing your cat all over the place)
- A non-slip surface
- A comfortable work height for you

For wet baths, use a bath or sink which can comfortably accommodate a cat. A deep kitchen sink or a baby bath is ideal.

Hair dryer/ blow dryer

There are many different types but you must be sure that airflow is not strong and the air is room temperature, no hotter. *The cat can be overheated, and can have a stroke or heart attack!*

Nail/claw clippers

There are many different types, styles and brands of nail/claw clippers available on the market: guillotine, scissors, small and large nail clippers, and even electric ones! You just need to find the ones you like.

Small scissor styles are great for kittens and small cats, large nail clippers ideal for larger cats with stronger claws; clippers with a long handle will give you extra distance if you need to keep your hands away from sharp teeth.

Blow dryer

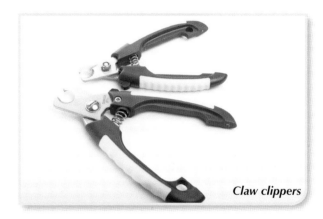
Claw clippers

No matter what your personal preference, it is absolutely essential to use sharp, good quality clippers. So, you can clip the claws sufficiently without splitting or cracking them.

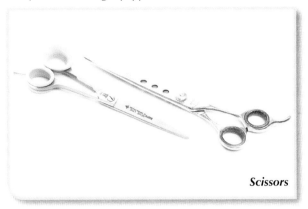

Scissors

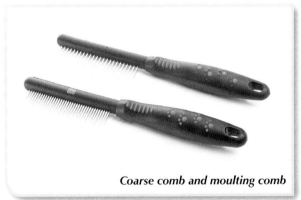

Coarse comb and moulting comb

Slicker brush

Combs and brushes

It's easy to get lost here! There are hundreds if not thousands available these days but it is not that complicated when you know what you're looking for.

The price range varies wildly, and it's a good lesson to learn that higher price does not necessarily mean better quality, and often the more expensive ones are less practical.

For example, a beautifully crafted horsehair bristle brush does a fantastic job without breaking the hair, but it's very hard to clean and almost impossible to get rid of the hair. If you are a professional cat groomer, this product is impractical when you have to clean and disinfect brushes thoroughly after each cat. And even if it's your own cat, you really need products that you can keep sparkling clean and disease-free.

For longhaired cat grooming you should only need two types of comb:

- Coarse comb for thicker coats – it has one row of wide teeth and will easily enter the coat
- Moulting comb for thinner coats – it has two rows of teeth, like the coarse comb but with a second row of shorter teeth interspersed, to pick up dead and unwanted hair.

And for the blow-dry and finishing:

- Soft-pin, small-sized slicker brush – this helps to separate the hairs while you blow dry, it speeds up the drying, traps any fluff and adds volume to the coat. [Note that the slicker brush may not be suitable for show quality cats.]

Whatever you choose, it's very important that the combs and brushes are highly durable, as you will be using them day in, day out and disinfecting them after each use. It is good practice to have enough combs and brushes ready to use for the whole day – as a professional, you will need a clean set for each cat you see. So for example, if you have six cats booked in, make sure you have six sets of brushes ready, and you can disinfect them all together at the end of the day. Make life easy for yourself!

We cannot over-emphasise the importance of hygiene in cat grooming. It is absolutely essential to use clean, disinfected combs and brushes on a cat! They may have skin infections and invisible fungi such as ringworm – that you may not even be aware of – which can be spread across equipment, between animals and even onto yourself.

If you are finishing with a wet bath, you will also need:

- *Bath or large sink*
- *Shower head or water bucket*
- *Suction cup and noose*
- *Non-slip mat*
- *Shampoo*
- *Towels*
- *Hair dryer/blow dryer*
- *"Third arm"*

Conditioning, detangling and tea tree sprays

A spray will help condition the hair when grooming, and prevent the hairs from breaking. Sprays will also help to keep the fluff from going everywhere when dry grooming. There are a number of good ones to consider:

- Conditioning sprays soften and moisturize the coat, and are the most popular.
- Detangling sprays help to tease out knots in particularly matted hair.
- A tea tree spray is great for soothing skin problems and killing off ectoparasites.

Please note that we are using Tea Tree spray which is safe to use on cats and not Tea Tree oil.

Shampoos

No matter how knowledgeable you are (spotting fleas is not rocket science!) by law you are not allowed to tell the owner that their cat has fleas. This is considered a diagnosis which, as a groomer, you are not allowed to make. You can tell the owner that you saw something that "looked like" fleas, and therefore used a tea tree shampoo!

You can use either non-diluted or diluted shampoo – both are fine, just always read the labels and make sure you have the right concentration. The shampoos listed below are some good options to consider. We recommend that you don't use washing up liquid when washing your cat, as it strips the hair of essential oils and is very abrasive.

Oatmeal shampoo. This is the most popular and all-purpose shampoo. Gives a good deep clean, it is great for sensitive skin and dry coats – also good on dandruff!

Brightening shampoo. Adds a glossy sheen to the coat, and brightens white fur in particular.

Moisturising shampoo. This is a really thick, rich shampoo for very dull or dry coats. It's seriously moisturising, but it takes forever to blow dry the cat afterwards so leave it to dry naturally!

Tea tree shampoo. This is a fantastic antiseptic and although it isn't an official flea treatment it has the added advantage of killing fleas instantly! And it is an excellent and safe conditioner for all cats.

Coat conditioning rinse

A conditioning rinse adds a great extra level of silkiness and moisture to the coat, and keeps the coat tangle free for longer. Use it if the cat is happy to spend a bit more time in the water. Do bear in mind they are designed to keep in moisture, so it will take longer to dry the cat.

Whatever shampoo you choose, it must be designed specifically for cats. It is essential to choose a top quality shampoo, so you can use it safely on the whole face, including the delicate nose and eye area.

Don't cut corners with a cheap shampoo! We even hear of people using washing up liquid! Cheap shampoos and detergents will strip the coat of its essential natural oils.

A healthy coat provides vital protection against bad weather, skin problems and infections.

Suction cup and noose

Towels

Ear, eye and body wipes

Suction cup and a noose.

If you are doing a wet bath and the cat is prone to wriggling around and trying to get out of the bath, a noose is a humane way of keeping him in position so that you can wash him with both hands. The suction cup sticks onto the side or the bottom of the bath so you can position it comfortably. It's very important when you're shopping for a noose to by one that has a lead long enough for the cat to have his head in a comfortable position – too short and he will be pulled into a crouching position (not very nice), too long and he'll be able to wriggle! You can find these in pet grooming supplier magazines and stores.

Towels

We find that microfiber towels are the best as they are incredibly absorbent – so kitty doesn't stay wet for very long – and they are soft, and can handle a lot of washing.

Cleansing wipes

There are lots of different varieties of ear and eye wipes and body wipes made for cats. Find one that you like, but avoid using human body or face wipes, or baby wipes, as they are too oily.

Setting the Scene

The room does not need to be very large. Some cats can be difficult to handle and may not like to be on a table. They may jump off, and run away to hide from you, so you don't want to be chasing them all over the place.

However it should be spacious enough to work safely with all the equipment you require to complete the grooming session. It is advisable to keep all wires and obstacles from the floor, to prevent trip hazards while you move around your room.

It is important to make sure that the room is secure, that the cat cannot escape and that you cannot be disturbed by customers or other staff while you are working. You want to be working in a calm, peaceful and happy environment, preferably without interruption from outside or from phone calls.

It is good to introduce cats to grooming from an early age

Some gentle soft background music may also help to keep things relaxed.

The room needs to be well lit, well ventilated, with climate control so that your cat doesn't get overheated. The room needs to be cleaned thoroughly, it should be vacuumed and the floor washed every day.

High hygiene standards are essential to avoid cross contamination between animals, so make your room easy to keep clean, with unfussy worktops and plinths on floor cupboards so that cats cannot hide underneath them.

Make sure that you have plenty of brushes and tools sanitised in advance. It is very important to make your cat grooming room ready for each arrival.

If you keep your cat in a spacious cat cage please do not forget to put in a nice clean blanket, bowl of fresh water and clean litter tray.

Bonding with your cat

Chapter 3

Before you start grooming, it is absolutely crucial to establish
a good relationship between you and the cat, and this fact
must not be underestimated!

Anita

Talking to your cat

Your first communication starts when you greet the cat with a soft, calm and soothing voice. Ask him how is he today and let him know that you're his friend.

It is essential to maintain a loving relationship from start to finish, and it is in your hands to make this experience pleasurable and trusting. It may not be as easy as it sounds but with great patience everyone can learn to trust, and cats are no exception.

By listening and talking to your cat and by tuning into his temperament, you will be able to predict and address his responses to different parts of the grooming process.

Give your cat a chance to relax and accept you, so he is comfortable and happy with you.

As you continually talk to and reassure the kitty, introduce your hands with very gentle movements starting from the favourite parts of his body: head, cheeks, neck, then shoulders and further back to the more sensitive areas; the back legs, belly and the tail.

Always begin by talking to the cat, one to one, in a soothing voice, whilst caressing his head, cheeks and chin, working your hands along the length of his body as you speak.

There are millions of different ways to talk to your cat, and he may talk back to you!

So learn his language too, and respond to his behaviour – always reward good behaviour with speech and touch but don't be afraid of adopting a louder and more assertive tone, if he challenges your authority.

Body Language

Hold your cat close to you and stroke him gently, concentrating behind his ears, on his head and under his chin. Talk to him in a low, gentle voice.

Tell him what a good boy he is. Take your time and don't rush him. Some cats will take longer to calm down than others, just give him what he needs.

If you are relaxed and willing to be patient, he will react well to you and trust you.

Holding the cat close to you throughout the grooming sends a clear message to him about your presence.

Enjoy being a Cat Whisperer, the secret of good bonding and indeed any loving and respectful relationship between people and cats!

Edita

No matter how well you learn the brushing and clipping techniques, if you do not build this connection and bond with your cat, he will never let you do the job.

Be calm and maintain your calm and reassuring voice during the whole grooming process, finishing it with a lots of wonderful warm words, hugs, kisses and cuddles!

Your calm and gentle approach with slow movements will create a great bond and build mutual trust between the two of you.

It gives you more control so you can sense the cat better and will be able to spot if he is growing restless and anxious – cats can be furious creatures and you don't want to get on the wrong side of them!

With the right bond you will be able to work alone and groom and handle the cat from start to finish without any help from another friend or colleague – which is really valuable, as you won't need to employ an extra person to assist you.

Sharon

Egle

Claw clipping

Chapter 4

Anatomy of the Claws

The claw is clear-coloured and made of a hard protein called keratin. The claw is arched in shape, curving downwards from the end of the last digit. (Diagram 1)

In the centre of the claw runs a strip of blood vessels, nerves and new keratin cells responsible for the growth, called the quick. It is pink and very sensitive and will bleed if you cut it.

Therefore, clip the claws no closer than 3–5mm from the quick keeping your nail/claw clippers at about 45° to the paw pad. (Diagram 2)

The claw is attached to the end of the last bone of the toe. There are five toes and five claws including a dewclaw on the front feet, and four toes with four claws on the back.

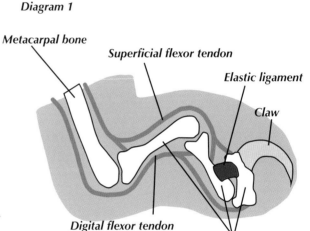

Diagram 1

Metacarpal bone

Superficial flexor tendon

Elastic ligament

Claw

Digital flexor tendon

Phalanges

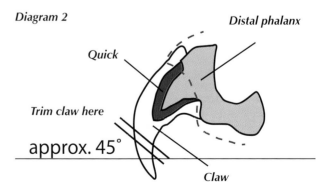

Diagram 2

Distal phalanx

Quick

Trim claw here

approx. 45°

Claw

Occasionally you may come across cats with a greater number of toes and claws. These are known as Polydactyl cats. This is a generally harmless condition, although the claws can sometimes grow and shed abnormally.

Purpose

The claws are versatile and multi-purpose tools for the cat. They are curved and pointed, and look like a hook with a needle-sharp tip, designed to allow the cat to grip and retain its grasp on its prey. It is also the cat's first line of defence against predators.

Keeping them trim

The claws grow constantly, with each fresh layer pushing up from the quick, much like the structure of growth in an onion.

As its claws grow, the cat needs to shed the old, dead top layers to reveal the new pin-sharp claw that lies underneath. Cats do this:

- on the front feet, by scratching them against a rough surface,
- on the back feet, by chewing off the outer layers of the claws

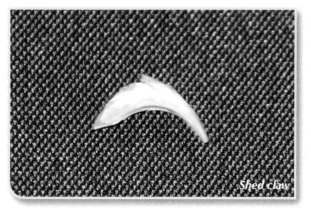

Shed claw

Scratching

Scratching is a natural process and an essential part of the cat's life. It not only helps to keep its claws in good and healthy condition, but it provides vital exercise for keeping the back muscles, shoulders and fore-limbs strong.

Do you need to clip the claws?

Outdoor cats will look after their claws themselves, but as they get older or become sick they will find it harder to do. If a cat is unable to maintain his claws by scratching, the claws will continue to grow, curling back under the paw, and will eventually penetrate the paw pad. This is extremely painful, and causes huge discomfort and inflammation – it is crucial to check the claws to make sure this doesn't happen.

Some owners may find that their cat plays too roughly and scratches them badly by accident, or that they simply want to keep their cat's claws trimmed and in good condition.

Whatever the reason, there is a comfortable and easy way to clip claws, pleasant for both you and the cat!

As a professional groomer, you have the right to refuse to groom a cat with unclipped claws. Some customers may want to keep the claws untouched, as they feel their cat needs them to climb trees. However, it is at your discretion whether you agree to groom the cat, just remember that it is your hands that you might be putting in danger! You can offer to see how it goes, but say that you will have to clip just the very tip if you think its necessary.

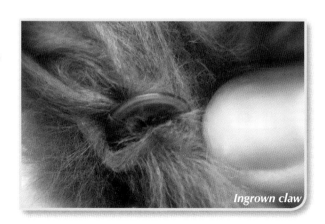

Ingrown claw

Claws Summary

Appearance:
- Five claws on the front foot and four claws on back foot
- Clear coloured
- Curved, pointed and needle-sharp
- Have a very sensitive "quick"
- Made of keratin, and growing constantly

Used for:
- First line of defence
- Catching and killing prey
- Digging and climbing
- Stretching and making muscles strong
- Destroying your furniture

Need clipping because:
- Old and infirm cats can't look after them
- Some cats scratch too boisterously
- Some clients will like their claws to be nice and trimmed regularly
- It will add greater protection for you if you are doing a full grooming

Diagram 3

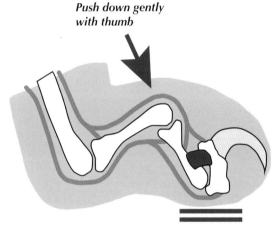

Push down gently with thumb

Support underneath paw pad with fingers

Clipping the Claws

The tools:

• One pair of claw clippers

Technique

You do not want to move your kitty too much unnecessarily, move yourself around kitty when you need to.

Front paws:

1. Position your cat on the table in front of you, his head facing to the right. Lean his body against yours, make sure he is comfortable and relaxed. (Figure 1)

2. Pick up his front left paw with your left hand, thumb on top, fingers and palm underneath. (Diagram 3 on p40) Use the whole length of your left arm to control him. (Figure 2)

3. Take the claw clippers in your right hand over his head and neck. You can control his movements by adding or releasing pressure to his neck with your right arm, and using the outside part of the right hand to control his head. (Figure 3)

Fig. 1

Fig. 2

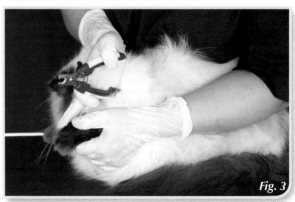

Fig. 3

Fig. 4

Fig. 5

Fig. 6

4. Keep your hands a good distance and away from his mouth and work from behind his head – remember they have very sharp teeth and even good kitties may bite!

5. Start with the dewclaw. As it is tucked under the side of the paw, it is the hardest claw to find, especially in long-haired cats. You can also use the right middle finger to rub under the paw to find it, it should snag on your glove. (Figure 4)

6. Use your left thumb to press on the joint where the claw attaches to the toe, holding the paw underneath with the rest of your palm. The claw will pop out. (Figure 5)

7. Hold the claw firmly so it is under your control and the cat can't jerk it away while you're cutting. (Figure 6)

8. Before you clip make sure you have a clear view of the whole claw to avoid any accidents and clipping too short (if you do clip too short by accident, see p.48). Use the thumb and fingers on your left hand to pull back any fur. Make sure you can see the "quick" of the claw. Long-haired cats have a lot of fur around their paws in general, which makes the claws hard to spot in the first place.

9. Cut off the sharp tip – you can take more of the claw off, but leave at least a 3–5mm gap from the quick. (Figure 7)

10. Keep your clippers vertical, and at a slight angle towards the paw pad. (Figure 8)

11. If you look over the top of the claw you will notice that it is narrower from side to side and is wider from top to bottom. Clip the claw straight up, with a clean vertical cut and not diagonally across. This will keep the claw from splitting.

12. Proceed to the next claw on the left front paw. It is good practice to move systematically around the paw, it will help the process become a habit and it ensures that you are thorough – it is easier than you think to miss one out!

    When you have finished this paw, praise your cat!

13. Move to the front right side. The cat stays in the same position, control the cat's body with your left arm and use your left wrist to control his head. (Figure 9)

    Use the same technique, working around the paw systematically in the way you prefer.

Fig. 7

Fig. 8

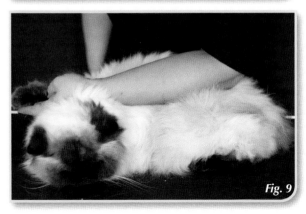

Fig. 9

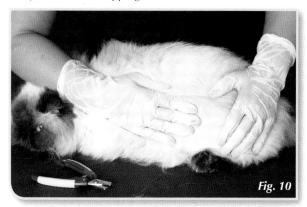

Fig. 10

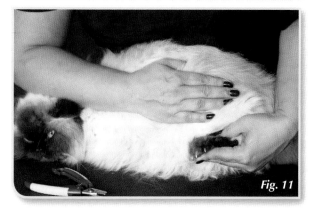

Fig. 11

Fig. 12

Back paws

Top Tip: Cats do not like to be touched around the rear parts of the body, especially the back feet, so it's more of a challenge to clip his back claws. You want to work as quickly as possible, while still being safe and doing a thorough job.

1. The cat is in the same position as for his front legs. Start with the left back leg. The clippers are in your right hand – use the length of your right arm to control the cat's body. (Figure 10)

2. Slide your left hand along his outer leg from hip to paw, finishing with his heel in the palm of your hand, and your fingers and thumb holding the foot. This way you have good control of the whole leg. (Figure 11)

3. Pick up the paw with the left hand, moving it slightly up and forward. Keep his paw as close to his body as possible, at the same time making sure that you have a clear view of the paw and claws.

4. The technique is now the same as for the front paws. Pull back any fur with your left thumb and press in at the toe joint to reveal the claw.

5. Hold the clippers in a vertical position, angled slightly towards the paw pad. Clip off the sharp tip, and getting no closer than 3–5mm from the quick. (Figure 12)

6. Systematically work around the paw. Count off each claw as you do it, there are should be four.

7. Clip the claws on his right back foot in the same way. Swap over the control to your left arm. The left arm comes over the back of the cat and holds the paw.

   Really try to keep him close to your body so that he can't wriggle. Alternatively, you could try sliding your left hand under his belly to pick up his right back foot. That way he is nicely in the crook of your arm and supported by your chest. (Figure 13)

8. Clipping the claws of the back feet can be quite uncomfortable for the groomer (Figure 14); the position is quite awkward as you don't have much control of the cat.

9. If you are having trouble, you can approach the claws from underneath, which gives a more comfortable angle – but be careful as there is a greater danger of accidently cutting his paw pads with the claw clippers. (Figure 15)

Fig. 13

Fig. 14

Fig 15

In our example we have described the routine from front to back, moving left to right, but it is not essential to follow us! You may have your own personal preferences and that is fine. As long as you create your own routine and stick it closely, you will not miss out any claws!

Whatever your personal preference for the order is, and which claw you like to start with – from inside out or outside in – the most important thing is that you build your routine day by day until it becomes habit and you know it by heart.

This way you work fast and efficiently, and never miss a claw!

What to do if you cut the claw to close to the quick and it bleeds.

It is very difficult cut the claw too short, however, accidents happen and we want you to know what to do in a very unlucky incident. Make sure that your emergency kit is always stocked up and close to hand.

Claw clipping summary

- Clipping the claws is not painful if you do it in the correct way.
- Try to move yourself rather than move the cat while you are working.
- Stay calm, talk to cat and give him plenty of reassurance. Praise him when the task is finished!
- Keep the cat close to your body. Use your body, arm and hands to help you to control the cat's movements.
- Pull the fur away from the paw so you can see the claw very clearly before cutting.
- Press on the top of the toe joint so the claw pops out
- Hold the paw firmly while clipping the claw.
- Keep your claw clippers in a vertical position and slightly angled toward the paw.
- Cut no closer than 3-5 millimetres from the quick.
- Only clip the claw when you are 100% sure you can see or feel what you are doing.

In an emergency you may need:

- Cotton pad, cotton bud

- 3% - H2C2 hydrogen peroxide (fantastic disinfectant for minor cuts and stopping bleeding. It is cheap and sold in any pharmacy without prescription; it is also sold as 6% which is stronger, but you should have no need for this)

- Any coagulating powder, which quickly stems bleeding

What to do:

- First of all do not panic!

- The quick only has small blood vessels so it will not bleed heavily

- Wet a cotton pad with 3% hydrogen peroxide

- Apply to the claw and hold for a few seconds/minutes, the blood should stop quite quickly

- If it continues to bleed, clean again with H2C2 and apply coagulating powder with a cotton bud

Dry Grooming

Chapter 5

The products and tools:

- A coarse and/or moulting comb
- Detangling and/or conditioning spray

The technique

Visualise your cat in sections, so you can groom step by step and you're not going to miss any part out. By doing this you will avoid hurting him by pulling at big sections of hair.

Start grooming with the easiest parts, such as the head, neck and shoulders – most cats are used to being stroked here so they will feel comfortable and relaxed. These are your first steps to bonding with the cat too. Gradually work around the body from the shoulders, to the armpits, the belly, the inner and outer legs, the sides and finishing with the back and tail.

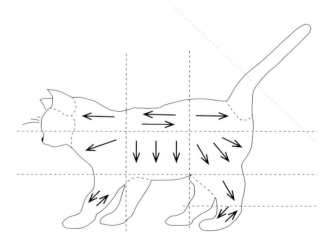

Detangling Spray

Detangling spray will help untangle knotted hair. When using detangling spray, particularly around the head and ears, try to keep it away from the sensitive eye area, nose and inner ears.

Spray 15-20cm away from the coat – they don't like the sound of the spray up close, and this will also diffuse the spray (better mist/all-over cover). If the cat is too frightened of the sound of the spray, apply the spray directly to the comb and away from the cat.

You don't want to move your cat too much, so in this guide we will talk you through each full side at a time.

Complete the grooming on the whole of the left side before moving the cat over onto his right side.

However, if your cat moves during the process, it's not the end of the world! You just need to remember which sections you need to finish as you go around.

Remember to brush only small portions at a time, working from the bottom to the upper parts. Keep your brush at a 45-degree angle down and away from you.

You will need short strokes to begin with to loosen the knots, then brush the hair through in long strokes – especially on the sides and belly where the hair is long.

Use the coat conditioner frequently to lightly moisten the hair (without getting it damp) to avoid breakage.

Always brush in small sections so as not to pull the hair and hurt the cat. Work your hands together with the comb, and keep your hands close together.

Use your left hand to control the cat and maintain a firm pressure to release small amounts of hair. Spray with the coat conditioner as needed.

The front of the cat: the head, chest and shoulders

1. The hair is short on the crown of the head, so use a moulting comb to brush in the opposite direction of the hair growth.

   Keep the comb at a 45-degree angle to the cat. (Figure 1)

Fig. 1

2. Move to the chest area: lift the head up (use your index finger in the groove in the middle of the lower jaw – this will make it easy to lift his head). (Figure 2)

   Still holding his head up with the finger you can add support of the hand below it.

   The fingers of your left hand also serve to hold back hair while you're brushing. (Figure 3)

Fig. 2

Fig. 3

Fig. 4

Fig. 5

3. Start at the bottom, and work up from the base/lower part of the chest. With the fingers (or the edge of the palm of the hand) hold up the hair. Release very small sections of the hair and comb downwards, away from the head.

   Try and keep a clean line so you can see what you're doing and not miss anything, and to be sure that it's not painful or unpleasant for him too (large sections would pull the hair). (Figure 4)

4. Now move round to the shoulder. Visualise the line where you finished the chest and start at the following point around the side. Repeat the same brushing process, starting low down the shoulder moving up towards the head. (Figure 5)

Never force the cat, always work with him not against him!

The underside of the cat: the armpits, belly and inner-legs

To groom the armpits and belly, you need to move the cat onto his side. Some cats are very cooperative and you can roll them completely onto their side, working on the full length of the belly.

Fig. 6

Technique for lifting and turning the cat onto his side

The cat is currently lying flat on his belly on the table (Figure 6):

- Your right arm is supporting the top of the body, holding him in place.

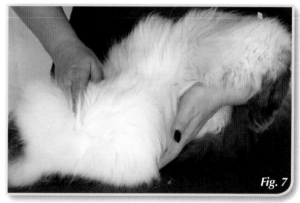

Fig. 7

- Slide your left hand between his back legs. Move your arm forwards towards the head and take hold of the front left leg. (Figure 7)

- You can now use the crook of your left elbow to hold up the left back leg. (Figure 8)

Fig. 8

Fig. 9

Fig. 10

Fig. 11

- Now your right arm is free. Use it to come behind the cat's right shoulder to the right paw. (Figure 9)

- Lift the upper body and leg, and twist forward, working with the left hand.

  Your left arm is controlling and moving the body, to make sure the cat doesn't try to twist back. (Figure 10)

- Now he is on his side, it is crucial not to let him go; don't be afraid to be a bit more firm.

  Stretch his head out in line with his body using your right hand and keeping your pinkie finger under his chin. (Figure 11)

  All this needs to happen quickly and firmly to hold him in this side position. Stretch his head out with your right pinkie finger, in line with the body.

  It's very important to keep your left hand in a firm hold of the body from now on, or he will naturally roll back onto his belly.

If they're not cooperative or they are extra large cats, you may have to do the underside of the cat in two or three sections, depending on the cat's flexibility and cooperation.

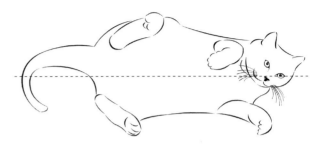

Diagram 1

First twisting the front legs and working under the armpits and belly, and then twisting the back legs to work on the rest of the belly and the inner-back legs.

You need to visualise the middle of the cat's belly so that you can work from the middle line, out and up, on each side.

(Follow diagrams 1 to 3 to see the process clearly.)

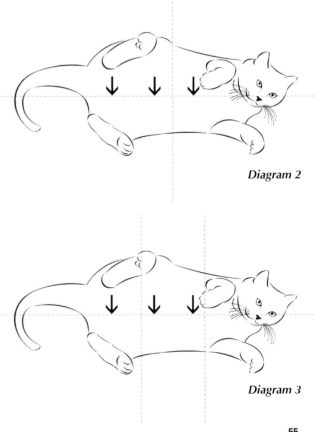

Diagram 2

Diagram 3

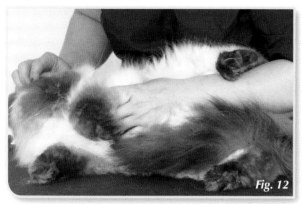

Fig. 12

Fig. 13

Grooming the armpits

1. With your left arm still supporting and controlling under the belly, use your left hand to lift the left front leg up. (Figure 12)

2. Take the comb in your right hand. Position it at a 45-degree angle facing away from you. Work from the visual middle line of the cat and up the leg towards the paw, lifting the leg higher as you move up. You can still control the cat's head with the pinkie finger of your right hand while you are combing. It will take some practice! (Figure 13)

3. Brush using small strokes and small sections, as always. And don't forget to talk to him!

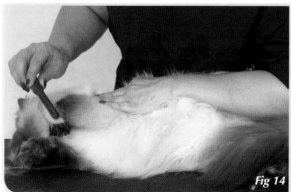

Fig 14

Fig. 15

4. While he is still in the same position, turn to the outer side of his front leg and brush it out, starting at the paw and working towards the shoulder. (Figure 14) Keep in mind the paws are sensitive, and they don't really like to be fussed with here.

5. As the hair on the legs is usually shorter than on the body, you can brush it in both directions. Start in the direction of the hair and then brush against the grain – it will give you better results. (Figure 15)

Grooming the belly and inner legs

1. Now the front left leg and armpit are groomed, bring the leg down but keep the cat in the same position. (Figure 16)

2. Work from your visual line along the middle of the cat upwards towards his back. Comb in small sections, line by line up the belly. (Figure 17)

3. Keep combing along the belly towards his back inner legs. While you do this, it is likely that the cat will roll the front half of his body forwards. This is fine, just keep your right elbow in control of his head. (Figure 18)

Fig. 16

Fig. 17

Fig. 18

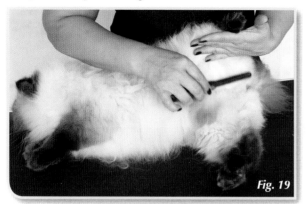

Fig. 19

4. Work from your visual middle line between the back legs, up the leg towards the paw. As you comb up the leg, slide your left hand up in unison with the brush strokes until you have stretched the whole leg out. Never force or yank the leg, always ask him to give it to you. (Figure 19)

Remember: a gentle approach
will give you his trust!

Fig. 20

5. While he is still on his side, do the outside and the back of the back leg too; it may be better to use a moulting comb on the shorter hair. You can brush the shorter hair in both directions for best results. (Figure 20)

The topside of the cat: the outer thigh and sides

As you continue, keep your cat lying on his side, and now onto his outer thigh. Comb from the paw towards the hip.

Fig. 21

1. Start with the lower part of the leg. The cat is still lying on his side. Hold the heel joint with your left hand, and extend slightly forward so you can brush easily. Brush in small sections from the paw upwards towards the knee, hip and his back. (Figure 21)

2. As you get to the knee, the coat is almost always thicker in this part of the body, so you may need a better grip on the hair – you may find it easier to hold the hair in a loose fist here; you can still release small sections of hair, but do not pull too hard. (Figure 22)

Fig. 22

3. Moving around the side of the cat the process is the same: start from the lower part of the side, working upwards from the visual middle line towards the back – make sure you really brush out each section before you move up. Keep brushing small sections in a clear line. (Figure 23)

Fig. 23

4. Now you are controlling the back of the cat with your left arm and elbow. The skin on his side is loose and will really sting if you pull it, so hold him close to you. Use long brush strokes to the ends of the hair, so it doesn't flick back and form new knots. (Figure 24)

Repeat the process on the other side. When it comes to turning the cat… there is no art form to this! Just pick him up and turn him around.

Carry out the grooming instructions in the same order but mirror your hand positions.

Fig. 24

A tip about grooming the backside

The majority of cats you meet will not like being groomed in this area.

Firstly, the hair is much thicker naturally, and because the owners are more likely to groom around the head this area is neglected.

Also, the cat will be unfamiliar with this new attention to a "private area"! He may be a bit restless, so you will need to be a bit firmer with him.

Always reassure him gently with your voice, and brush small portions at a time so you don't pull too hard.

To keep him in position, hold him close to your body so he can't move around much, and use the whole length of your right arm and elbow over the top of him.

Grooming the back and tail of the cat

The cat is now fully groomed apart from the back and the tail. For better results you may groom against the direction of hair growth. Divide your cat visually into two or three sections, for example into front, middle and back (Diagrams 1 – 2)

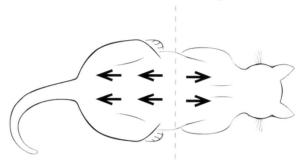

Diagram 1

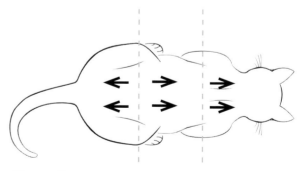

Diagram 2

Groom against the hair growth for one third or half of the cat. However, the hair is thicker towards the rear and it will be more unpleasant for the cat to do this.

It will also be more difficult to control the cat and you can over-brush him as well.

1. At the head, brush in the opposite direction to the hairs for best results. Use your left hand to support the cat and hold back the hair, releasing small sections as usual. (Figure 25)

2. As you move towards the tail you are losing more control of his front end and head. It's also more difficult to brush the longer hair at the back, particularly against the direction of hair growth.

   Change direction so your body is at the front end of the cat, and you can control his body with the length of your right arm and elbow. (Figure 26)

3. Brush in the direction of the hair now, starting at the base of the tail and moving towards the middle of the back until you have reached your middle line. (Figure 27)

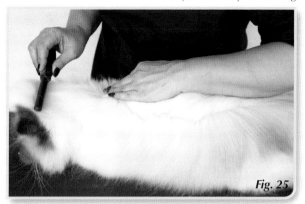

Fig. 25

Fig. 26

Fig. 27

Diagram 1

Fig. 28

Fig. 29

The tail is the most hated part!

1. Visually split the tail into two sections, one quarter and three quarters (see Diagram 1). The base of the tail can be brushed against the direction of the hair as it is fluffier. However when you brush the end three quarters of the tail, always go with the hair – you don't want to over-brush and make the tail look too thin.

2. Start by lifting under the base of the tail with your left hand, to groom his backside and under-tail (the quarter at the base of the tail). Groom gently in small sections away from you. Still working on the base, brush both sides, moving the brush outwards. (Figure 28)

3. Once you have finished all sides of the base of the tail, move to the tip (the end three quarters). Hold the bones of the tail in your left hand, don't grip too tightly but use your fingers to tease out the hair along the length. Don't brush over the bones, this will hurt, use your fingers to control the hairs and brush in the direction of growth. (Figure 29)

Now you have groomed from head to tail. Finish with light brush strokes around his face and cheeks, as they all love it!

Cleaning the eyes, ears and nose

Chapter 6

At some point in the grooming you may like to clean the cat's face.

This can be done after the dry grooming using eye and ear wipes, if you are not going to go on to bath the cat.

If you are going to carry on with a wet grooming, this can wait until you have washed the cat and you can use a damp corner of the towel you dry him in to clean the face.

Products:

- Eye, ear and body wipes (or towel if after the wet bath)
- Cotton buds

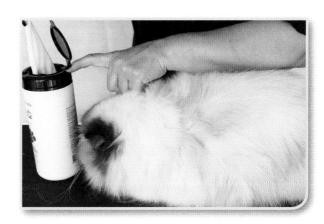

Fig. 1

Fig. 2

Fig. 3

Cleaning the eyes

1. Take a cleansing wipe and fold it around your thumb so you have a good cushion. (Figure 1)

2. With your other hand, place one finger under the chin so his mouth is closed, and place your thumb behind his head. This way, you will have good control.

3. Approach the corner of the eye with the wipe, starting at the top and wiping out in a gentle but firm stroke across the cheek (Figure 2)

4. Sweep across the eye in one movement. If there is still dirt in the eye, fold the wipe again so you have a clean section, and repeat the action. (Figure 3)

5. Do this until the eye is clean. Take a new wipe for the other eye, and repeat the process. A new, clean wipe will ensure there is no cross-contamination between the eyes.

Cleaning the ears

1. Face the cat. Hold up the ear between your thumb and first finger. (Figure 4)

2. Put your index finger on the back of the ear and push it forward, bending the tip of the ear backwards. You will now have a good view of the whole inner ear. (Figure 5)

3. Take a new cleansing wipe and wrap it around your thumb so that the layers form a soft pad.

4. There are lots of pockets in the ear, and the skin is very delicate, so make sure you use very, very gentle strokes. Clean only the area you can see, don't force your finger into the ear.

5. Use a scooping movement to collect the dirt around the bare skin outside the ear; stroke movements will spread the dirt across the cheek. (Figure 6)

6. Finally, if there is still dirt in the ear pockets, you can clean it out with soft cotton buds.

Fig. 4

Fig. 5

Fig. 6

Fig. 7

Fig. 8

Cleaning the nose

He may have dirt in his outer nostril.

1. Place the left hand around the head, with one finger holding up his chin and keeping his mouth closed. Your thumb holds the back of his head. (Figure 7)

2. Use a damp cotton bud to wipe away any visible dirt, using a twisting motion (Figure 8)

Finally, use a finishing wipe over the body to collect any fluff and loose hairs. Finish with a final few strokes with a comb to neaten the hair and complete your grooming.

Now give him a well-earned kiss and cuddle, and tell him how well he's done!

Wet Bath

The idea that cats don't like water would be a myth if we could only introduce them to water when they are kittens.

Introduce older cats to water slowly and in a gentle way and the majority will allow you to wash them without much grumbling, provided you don't squirt their faces.

It's crucial that you still complete the full dry grooming **first**, so that the hair is in good condition and all brushed out.

If you wet the hair before it has been brushed any knots and matted sections will tangle even more tightly; it will be far harder to wash out the products; and will be very painful for the cat if you try and brush out knots afterwards.

Products and equipment

- Shampoo
- Coat conditioner or rinse*
- Non-slip rubber mat
- Suction cup and noose
- A soft, absorbent towel

*optional

Types of bath

Whatever your preference for bathing your cat you must continue to reassure him

All the time talk to the cat in a calm, low voice – soothing and reassuring – so he knows he's safe and can trust you.

Each time he will be more trusting and happier in the situation.

There are a number of different ways to bath the cat. It depends what your cat prefers, for example he may be scared of the sound of the shower, so use a jug and bucket of water. Or some cats may not like being in a big pool of water, so a shower would be better for them.

It will take another book to explain all the different methods! We prefer the shower if possible, as the clean, running water gives the best results. This method is described below.

The technique

Talk to the cat throughout the whole grooming – it is really important to do this constantly during the bath, as this will be a completely foreign experience for most cats.

Placing the cat in the sink

1. Put a rubber mat in the bottom of the sink, so the cat has a good grip. Make sure the mat is not covering the open plughole, so the water can run freely.

2. The plughole is very important! You will need a plughole strainer cover so that the cat's toes don't get stuck in the open hole if he moves around. You may already have one in your house. This is particularly important in a small sink.

Fig. 1

3. Attach the suction cup (separate from the noose at this stage) to the bottom of the sink. If it is on the side it is easier to slip up if the cat pulls on it. (Figure 1)

4. Have the cat facing away from you – if he is facing you he will try and escape by climbing up you.

   Reassure him all the time – talk to him, stroke him and comfort him if he is anxious. (Figure 2)

Fig. 2

5. Now put the noose over his head, and make sure the padded part is under his chin.

   The noose should be a comfortable length, not strangling him – nooses come in different lengths so make sure you are using the appropriate one for you cat. (Figure 3)

6. Attach the noose to the suction cup.

Fig. 3

Fig. 4

Fig. 5

Fig. 6

Bathing/showering the cat

1. Before you start to bath him, make sure the water is medium pressure – high pressure will be uncomfortable, frightening and painful for him.

   The water should be warm, and neither too hot nor cold.

2. The sudden sound of the shower may scare him.

   Prepare the cat for the shower by holding him firmly and speak louder to drown out the sound of the water coming on.

   Give him time to adjust to the sound of the water.

3. Start by wetting your hands and putting a little amount of water over the cat's head and face, and stroking his head. (Figure 4)

   Make sure he is completely adjusted to the shower before you carry on. (Figure 5)

4. Now you can introduce the shower head and soak the whole body, including the legs and tail. (Figure 6)

It is very important to never squirt the water directly into his face (use your hand to wash his face – see point 8)

5. Keep the showerhead close to his body. You can use the showerhead as an additional "arm" to support and control the cat better. (Figures 7, 8 and 9)

Also, the water pressure will be more pleasant for him if it is closer to his body. Gently tease the hair, as it will tangle easily.

Fig. 7

Fig. 8

Fig. 9

Fig. 10

Fig. 11

Fig. 12

6. Now you are ready to add shampoo. Keep the water running so the noise is consistent.

    Be generous with the shampoo, pouring plenty into your hands or directly onto the coat – you want to build a good lather. (Figure 10)

7. Apply shampoo all over the body, starting at the head and moving over the shoulders, belly, legs and tail, so the shampoo can start to work while you go back to massage each area.

8. Start with the head and face. Hold the head with both hands, simultaneously use your fingers to massage and control the chin, and use your thumbs to work in the shampoo on the top of his head.

    This takes some practice! (Figure 11)

9. Start at the back of the head and ears, gently spreading the lather forwards with your thumbs, down over the face.

    Never apply shampoo directly onto the eyes – gentle lather is OK. (Figure 12)

10. If your cat has very deep creases around the eyes (some Persians or exotic breeds may have these) you can use soft, soapy cotton pads for a deeper clean.

    Make the strokes from the inner corner of the eye, outwards. Always be very, very gentle – do not rub around the eye area.

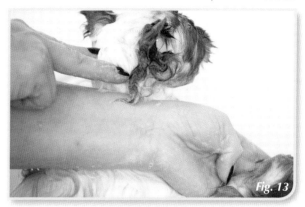
Fig. 13

11. A good quality shampoo will not irritate the cat's eyes. The shampoo is safe and you don't need to rinse off straight away, let it work to give a good deep clean on the face.

12. From the head move to the chest, front legs and paws. Keep the coat nice and wet so that the shampoo lathers. (Figure 13)

Fig. 14

13. Do the whole of the front leg, moving towards the paw. With your left hand, hold the cat's head up and away, and use your right hand to lift up the paw and simultaneously massage in the shampoo. Pay good attention to the paws, as they get so much use. (Figure 14)

14 Repeat the same process on the other front leg, switching your hands. (Figure 15)

Fig. 15

Fig. 16

Fig. 17

Fig. 18

15. Move to the middle section of the cat. Use the shower or fill your hands with a little water to loosen up the shampoo into a good lather. Massage his back with both hands.

16. Apply more shampoo to your hands and have a good scrub of the belly and sides.

17. Move to the hip area and start on one back leg at a time. You want your cat in a standing position if possible. Put your right hand under his bum, between his legs, and lift and hold him up.

    Use your left hand to shampoo the left outer thigh, moving towards the paw.

18. Slide your right hand further in between his legs, so he is almost sitting in the crook of your elbow, and shampoo the left inner thigh.

19. Repeat the process on the right back leg, switching your hands.

20. Now wash his bum and give his tail a good scrub. Your cat may not like you washing this area – it is his private parts after all. Work fast but sufficiently to get a thorough clean. (Figure 16)

21. Reapply and do a second bath if you think that the cat is still dirty. You will be able to tell – don't do a full rinse of the first shampoo, but wash most of it off and reapply and lather for a second time. Be sure then to rinse off all shampoo thoroughly.

22. If the cat is good and happy in the water, you can apply coat conditioner, from head to tail. Apply the conditioner using the same method as above.

23. Rinse thoroughly. (Figures 17–21)

24. Remove excess water with your hands, squeezing down the body and very gently on the tail. Gently remove the noose, wrap your kitty in a soft towel and bring him back to the grooming table.

Give him cuddles and tell him what a good boy he has been!

Fig. 19

Fig. 20

Fig. 21

Elvis, after his wet bath!

Drying the Cat

Chapter 8

Towel dry techniques

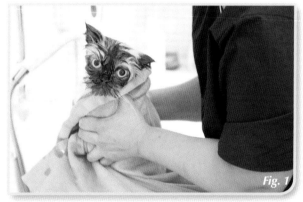

Fig. 1

1. Wrap the cat with the towel while he is in the sink before transferring him to the table. (Figure 1)

2. Your cat is now on the table. Gently rub and squeeze the hairs with the towel.

   It is OK to rub vigorously on the shorter areas of hair such as the paws and legs but with the longer sections work lightly squeezing rather than rubbing and only in the direction of the hair so you don't create knots. (Figure 2)

Fig. 2

Fig. 3

3. You can use a damp part of the towel to clean his ears – use the same technique as with the wipes in *Chapter 6: Cleaning the Eyes, Ears and Nose*. (Figure 3)

Avoid using a dry part of the towel, as this can damage the sensitive inner-ear skin.

Alternatively, you can use wipes. Any remaining dirt in the ear pockets can be cleaned with soft, good quality cotton buds.

Fig. 4

4. Have a quick look at his teeth just to check for any visible problems and bring any concerns to the attention of the owner so they can talk to their vet. (Figure 4)

5. Now you have got rid of the excess water, you can replace the wet towel with a new dry one for the blow dry. (Figure 5)

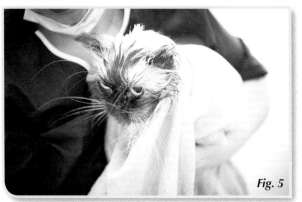

Fig. 5

After the bath, the wet hair sticks together so once you have given him a good towel dry, go over the coat very gently and quickly with the coarse comb to separate the hairs out.

Work in small sections at a time, in the direction of the hair (using the same techniques as the dry grooming), but with lighter and quicker strokes. (Figures 7–10)

For better results you can use the moulting comb on the short hair of the legs and a coarse comb on longer hair on the body.

Be careful of over-combing the hair when it is wet as this can be uncomfortable for the cat and can drag healthy hair from the coat as well.

Fig. 7

Fig. 8

Fig. 9

Fig. 10

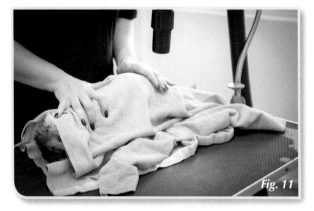
Fig. 11

Fig. 12

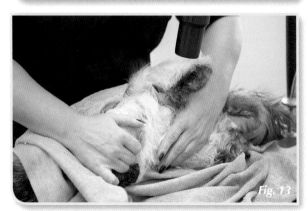
Fig. 13

Hand blow dry techniques

Now the cat is ready for the blow dry. Introduce the sound of the hair dryer gradually – cover the cat completely with the dry towel and hold him as he may jump up with the sudden sound of the hair dryer. (Figure 11)

Face the dryer away from the cat, give him a chance to adjust to the strange noise, talk loudly to drown out the sound, and to reassure him it's ok.

*If the cat is really scared by the hair dryer,
you can let him dry naturally, as long as you keep him
in a warm environment.*

Fig. 14

1. When blow-drying, start at the tail end – if you put the dryer straight in his face and ears, he'll be scared.

2. Pull back a little bit of the towel and concentrate first on the underside of the cat: inner legs, leg joints, belly and armpits – which are more time consuming to dry – followed by the shoulders and along the back. (Figures 12–16)

   The chest and face will be the last sections you come to. (Figure 17)

3. Use the same techniques described in the grooming chapter (*Chapter 5 - Dry Grooming*) – the process is done in the same order, working in small sections using the slicker brush.

   Use a very, very light stroke, you don't want to brush, just fluff the hair to help the air get through it. The teeth on the slicker brush can be very sharp and can scratch the delicate skin.

4. You can also use a coarse or moulting comb at your discretion. Just keep in mind that over-brushing your cat can make him bald, so judge carefully how much undercoat you want to remove.

Fig. 15

Fig. 16

Fig. 17

Fig. 18

Fig. 19

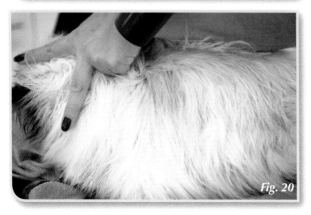

Fig. 20

5. When blow-drying longer hair keep the dryer further away from the area you are drying to avoid it curling back and becoming tangled. On the paws and forelegs you can afford to be closer to the fur as it is shorter. (Figures 18–19)

6. The head and face are always tricky to blow dry. Always blow dry from the back of the head towards the nose. Use the comb very carefully on his cheeks, as you are very close to his eyes. (Figure 18)

If you prefer, you can use your fingers instead – he might like this as it will remind him of strokes!

As a rule of thumb keep the hair dryer double the length of the hair you are drying away from the coat i.e. if the hair is 5cms long then have the dryer at least 10cm away from the cat's body.

Never dry directly into his eyes, nose and ears.

Re-affirming your Bond with the Cat

Chapter 9

Finishing Touches

Now he is fully dry, take a comb and style the hair back to his natural look. The basic job is done, with a "Natural Look" finish. Some owners like their cats to have a final trim around the paws, chest, backside, belly and "trousers". There are many styles to learn, each one requires skill and special techniques. We will be exploring these techniques and styles later in the series.

Dianne

Rachael

Sue

Jan

Liliana

At the end of grooming, leave him with a positive memory of the experience. Brush him out completely with gentle strokes finishing the whole grooming process with brushing the head and cheeks – his favourite parts.

Praise him for his patience and show him your love with strokes and cuddles.

Sandra

Carolyn